THE PROJECT MANAGER'S QUICK START GUIDE

HOW TO GET YOUR PROJECT ON THE RIGHT ROAD FOR SUCCESS!

Jon McGlothian

TMOG, LLC | PO 56415
VIRGINIA BEACH, VA 23456

The Project Manager's Quick Start Guide

by Jonathan T. McGlothian, Sr

Copyright © 2016 Jonathan T. McGlothian, Sr

Published by SkillBites LLC

All rights reserved.

ISBN-10: 1-942489-25-0

ISBN-13: 978-1-942489-25-2

CONTENTS

DEDICATION

With grateful thanks to God, I dedicate this writing to my faithful and loving wife, Tracy McGlothian, and in memory of my father, Rev. Dr. Odell McGlothian, Sr.

PREAMBLE

This is a quick start guide on how to manage your projects. It is not meant to be an all-inclusive guide; rather, it is designed to enable you as a newly appointed leader of a project to quickly organize your thoughts so that you can successfully launch a project, develop a plan for success, and lead the team to a successful project close. You may have found yourself being assigned a tasking by your supervisor, and the tasking may be to work on a project that is outside of your comfort zone. Oftentimes, this is seen as a stretch assignment for you so that you can expand your capacity and capabilities. Over the years, I have worked with many individuals who were suddenly given projects to execute and therefore became de facto project managers by accident. If the person was successful in delivering this assignment, they often became the "go to" person for these special projects. They became successful because they were quickly able to develop a systematic way to manage and lead projects, even when the projects were outside of their known expertise.

Think of the following scenario: Your boss gives you a call asking you to take on a highly visible effort for the organization. In this case, the boss has asked you to spearhead an internal conference for the senior leadership teams of several divisions within the organization. You are really excited to have been given this opportunity, as it means you will have a chance to showcase your skills and talent—a game-changing career move. However, you are a little concerned, as it also means that if it does not go well, you may suffer a damaging blow to your career. So this is a high-stakes effort to you and the organization.

At first you are really excited and then reality steps in. You realize that you have never spearheaded this type of effort before. You are smart and talented, but up until now you have dealt with issues and concerns that were clearly in your area. Now you are being asked to step outside of your comfort zone and actually work with individuals from across the organization on a task where you are not the subject matter expert.

These types of scenarios happen all of the time. One of the keys to success is to adopt a project manager's mindset. But in order to adopt this mindset, you have to recognize that you have been given a project. In its simplest form, a project has a start date, an end date, and a unique deliverable. In this scenario, the boss has a given you a large-scale tasking that you need to complete. This particular tasking meets all of the criteria to be a project. The start date is the beginning of the conference; the end date is the end of the conference. While this conference has been done before, it will involve different individuals and has a different goal; therefore, it has a unique deliverable. Thus, this is a project.

KICK-OFF PROCESS

The first step is to develop a *charter*. Before you can expend resources on the project, you need to have the authority to do such. The charter gives you the authority to expend your organization's resources. Typically, the person who is financially obligating the required resources will provide the charter. This person is known as the *sponsor*. In this scenario, your boss is the sponsor.

Hopefully, your sponsor through the charter provides enough information so that you know what direction to head as well as the desired end state. It is possible that your sponsor won't be able to provide the needed detail. In this case, the first part of the project may be to develop the charter. Also, the charter should be able to last the entire project; therefore, if the charter changes, one may have to consider terminating that project and beginning another.

Here are some key questions that the charter should answer:

Why are we doing this project? In any leadership situation, one of the most important issues that the leader must understand and be able to convey is, why are we doing this? It is important to determine the legitimacy and importance of the project before you begin. Running projects is very challenging and can become very frustrating. But understanding the "why" behind the project helps you and the team to stay focused on the big picture during the project.

Who is paying for this project, and what is the budget? The person or entity that is paying for the project ultimately has the final say on the budget (and whether the bills will be paid). The budget also helps to determine the level of importance as well as the quality expectations. For example, if a sponsor says that he or she wants a "steak dinner" but is only willing to pay for a "hamburger dinner," the differences need to be worked out early on. Now, it is possible that the sponsor may not know how much the project will cost and therefore what the budget will be. In this case, the initial phase of the project may be to determine the budget.

Is there any preliminary guidance? Is there a roadmap as to how this project will be delivered? Most of the time, a person is selected to manage the project well after the project has begun, so the initial groundwork may have already been done and approved. If this is the case, then you need to know this so that you do not have to reinvent the wheel or go down a path that the organization has already deemed unsuitable. If this is not the case, another part of the initial phase may be to determine the roadmap or strategy for achieving the goals.

Who are the stakeholders? Who will be impacted and who needs to know? While your stakeholders list will continue to grow and be refined throughout the project, you need to find out on the onset who is going to be impacted by the project, who needs to know about the project, and who is potentially against the project. From there, you need to develop strategies to be able to work with them. Just remember that the strategies are intended to keep the project moving forward as well as to prevent the project from being derailed.

Who will be helping me? Basically, you are asking if there is a team already selected to help. If you are working in a large organization, you will probably not know who in the organization has the skill sets and willingness to help you. Your sponsor should help you identify the individuals who will initially be on the team.

How will changes be made during the project? It is very rare for the project manager to have total authority on the project. Usually, the project manager will need to work with others to make and approve the changes to the project. It is important to identify who these individuals are early on; these individuals will become members of your *change control board*. The change control board is the entity that is authorized to make changes on the project.

What does success look like? A picture of what the physical project may look like at the end is helpful. You are asking what the goals and intentions of the project are. This is important, as you need to know what the end state will look like when the project is complete.

When is the project expected to be completed? The sponsor should set forth the timeline and the expectations for when the project should be completed.

These are some of the key questions that you need to know before embarking on your project. Again, if your sponsor cannot provide the answers to the questions, the first part of the project may have to be spent determining what the answers are.

Here is what a sample charter may look like for the scenario given earlier:

Sample Charter

The purpose of this project is to hold a conference in our city for the corporate office. Our division will fund the project. We expect sixty individuals to attend and the budget should not exceed $75,000. We want the individuals to come away from the conference knowing the organization's goals and objectives for the year. The key stakeholders are the president of the company and the corporate committee. Attendees include the leadership teams from all six of our divisions. As the project manager, you will need to create the plan to keep them up to date, and they need to know key details three to six months out so that they can plan their schedules. Mike from Engineering and Angela from Operations will be available to help. We did this type of affair about four years ago and Jack was in charge of it. Please let me as the sponsor know if there are any changes as you go through the planning process.

Signed, "Boss"

While this is a very short charter, it does provide enough detail for you as the project manager to begin planning the project. Depending on your actual scenario and organizational culture, your charter may be much longer and more detailed. The key is to write it in such a way that the project team knows what the scope is and what the broad parameters are.

As you get an idea of whom the stakeholders are, you will need to create a *communications plan* to keep them informed. The following format is a good way to organize your thoughts. Keep in mind that this plan will change as new stakeholders are added or as stakeholders' roles change. (Also, if you want a set of additional project templates, go to **www.tmogllc.com/PMQuickStart**.)

Column A	Column B	Column C	Column D	Column E
Stakeholder	What information do they need to know?	How often do they need an update?	Who on the project team will deliver the reports?	How will the information be delivered?
President of the company (Luke)	Will we be ready on time?	Weekly	The project manager	Via e-mail unless there is a significant issue, and then a face-to-face meeting will be scheduled
Mike (from Engineering) and Angela (from Operations)	They may want to know how they can assist.	Daily (since they are a part of the team)	The project manager	Face-to-face meetings
Corporate Committee Members (Jack, Mary, Larry)	Are my agenda items noted in the itinerary?	Weekly	The project manager	Via e-mail unless there is a significant issue, and then a face-to-face meeting will be scheduled
Your boss	Are there any problems that will derail this effort?	Daily	The project manager	Via e-mail unless there is a significant issue, and then a face-to-face meeting will be scheduled

FIGURE OUT THE SCOPE

After you have been issued the charter and therefore authorized to begin work, you need to begin determining the *scope*. The scope defines what you are actually doing and in some cases what you are not doing. The goal is to develop a set of deliverables called *work packages* that represent the entire project. The sum of all of the deliverables should equal the totality of your project so that 100 percent of the work packages equals 100 percent of the project. In order to create these work packages, you need to know what the requirements are so that you can tie each work package to a requirement.

You begin with developing and understanding the requirements. Using the list of stakeholders that you developed earlier, you will begin to interview those stakeholders so you can create and organize the requirements. An example of a requirement may be that the event site for the conference must hold at least 60 people and have easy access to hotel rooms for those who have to fly in and stay overnight. Then, you want to start decomposing your project into work packages. Decomposition is a powerful technique that enables you to take a complicated project and break it down into smaller, more manageable pieces. For illustrative purposes, below is an example of a *work breakdown structure* (WBS) for the conference that you have been placed in charge of. You can either present the WBS as a graphical representation or in an outline form. Remember that a work package is not a list of activities but rather the lowest level of detail that represents a deliverable. In some cases, the work package may become a project for the owner of the work package.

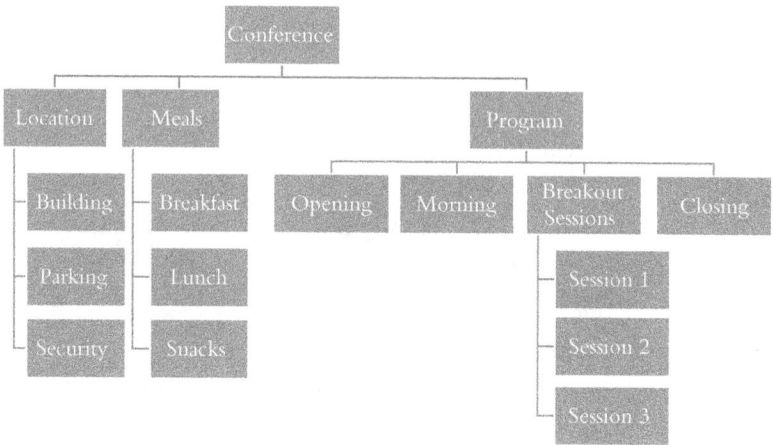

Conference

1. Location
    1.1. Building
    1.2. Parking
    1.3. Security
2. Meals
    2.1. Breakfast
    2.2. Lunch
    2.3. Snacks
3. Program
    3.1. Opening Program
    3.2. Morning Program

3.3. Breakout Sessions
    3.3.1. Breakout Session 1
    3.3.2. Breakout Session 2
    3.3.3. Breakout Session 3
3.4. Closing Program

During this process, you need to tie your requirements list to your WBS (work breakdown structure).

Stakeholder Originator	Requirement	Work Package Disposition
Jack	Have a program with opening, morning, closing, and breakout sessions	Fulfilled by 3.1, 3.2, 3.3 and 3.4 (Program)
Mary	Be sure to have adequate meals planned for the conference	Fulfilled by 2.1, 2.2, 2.3 (Meals)
Larry	Have the conference at an offsite location that is convenient to everyone with adequate parking and security	Fulfilled by 1.1, 1.2, and 1.3 (Location)

The goal is to make sure that each requirement is addressed by a work package. If a work package is not addressing a requirement, then you have two choices. If it is a legitimate oversight, then you can create a requirement. The other option is not to include the work package if it does not have anything to do with your project. It is also helpful to note what success looks like for each package.

After you get to a stopping point, you may want to review with your preliminary team and your sponsor for additional thoughts and guidance. After you have reached an agreement, this WBS becomes your *scope baseline*. The scope baseline represents all of the work that is to be done by the project. In this scenario, the work packages are the building, parking, security, breakfast, lunch, snacks, opening program, morning program, breakout session 1, breakout session 2, breakout session 3, and closing program. The sum of all of these work packages equals the entire project. Furthermore, each work package fulfills a specific requirement. It is not unusual to go through several iterations until all of the work packages are identified, making sure that all of the requirements can be satisfied by the work packages.

Any changes after this point need to go through the change control board that was established earlier. In this scenario, your boss is the change control board, as noted in the charter.

CREATE A WINNING TEAM

Creating a team is both an art and a science. On a personal basis, I firmly believe that the best training grounds to learn how to establish a team is in a volunteer setting. After all, if you can get people excited to work on a project that they are not being paid for, imagine what you can do with folks who are both excited about the work and are getting paid for it. In short, the best way to pull your team together is to rally them around "why" you are doing this tasking. This should look familiar, as it was a part of your charter. Even if your team has been preassigned—meaning that they were "told" that they are to help out—it is still your responsibility to create a vision and help them to understand the "why" behind the project. Your WBS will also give you a very clear picture of the types of team members that you will need to have on your team. So look at your WBS and use it to start building your team.

When you do have your team members on board, be sure to find out when they are not available to work on your project. Examples of not being available include vacation time and other work commitments. If their availability will not meet the needs of the project, you may have to look for other options. It is also critical to let the team members know what success looks like for their work packages. In some cases, the work package may become a project for the *responsible individual* (project team member) and you will need to let him or her know what the quality expectations are for that particular work package. In most cases, you do want to have some sort of a team-building exercise so that each team member knows what the other team members' roles and responsibilities are for the project. Go to **www.tmogllc.com/PMQuickStart** for some additional ideas on team-building exercises.

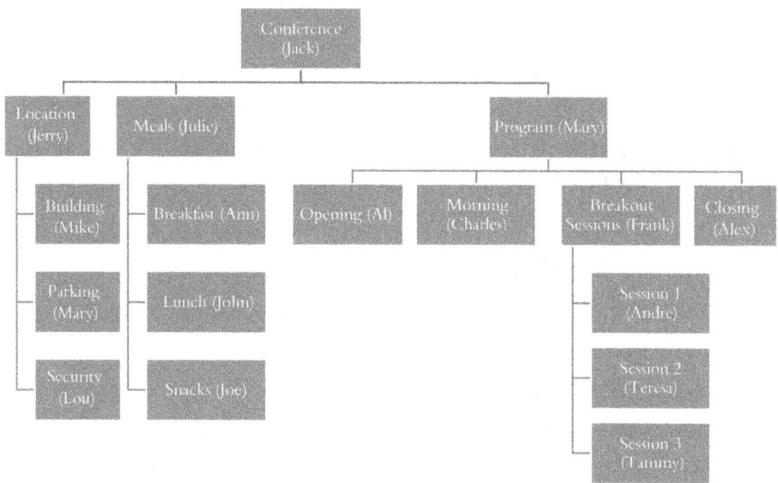

SCHEDULE THE WORK

Once you have identified all of the deliverables that are required to successfully complete the project, you now need to assign some due dates for the deliverables. One very straightforward way to do this is to place all of your work packages in a column and then note the due dates by each work package.

At this stage, you will have successfully tied the milestones from the WBS to the responsible project team member to the delivery dates.

Scope	Responsible Individual	Due Date
Building	Mike	January 15
Parking	Mary	January 20
Security	Lou	January 25
Breakfast	Ann	February 1
Lunch	John	February 1
Snacks	Joe	February 1
Opening Program	Al	March 1
Morning Program	Charles	March 1
Breakout Session 1	Andre	March 1
Breakout Session 2	Teresa	March 1
Breakout Session 3	Tammy	March 1
Closing Program	Alex	March 1

Now, we know that Mike—who is responsible for the building—is to have the building location secured by January 15. Do not be afraid to provide dates to your team. In the long run, it will help them to stay on track and give you confidence that everything is going well. Or, if dates are being missed, you can proactively provide corrective action to ensure that the overall project will succeed.

COSTING

Knowing how much the project will cost as well as when you will need to spend the funds on the project will be critical to the success of your project. One quick way of getting the costing together is to create a *cost estimate* for each work package. After you create the cost estimate for each work package, you can total the costs of all of the work packages to determine the overall cost of the project. The budget is simply taking the cost of each work package and noting when the funds will be used during the project. This should tie very closely to your delivery dates schedule.

Using the conference as an example, your cost structure may look like this:

Work Package	Cost Estimate	January	February	March
Conference (sum of Location, Meals, Program)	*$ 3,530*	*$ 1,600*	*$ 1,050*	*$ 880*
Location (sum of Building, Parking, Security)	*$ 1,600*	*$ 1,600*		
Building	*$ 1,000*	*$ 1,000*		
Parking	*$ 250*	*$ 250*		

Work Package	Cost Estimate	January	February	March
Security	$ 350	$ 350		
Meals (sum of Breakfast, Lunch, Snacks)	**$ 1,050**		**$ 1,050**	
Breakfast	$ 350		$ 350	
Lunch	$ 550		$ 550	
Snacks	$ 150		$ 150	
Program (sum of Opening, Morning, Breakout Sessions, and Closing)	**$ 880**			**$ 880**
Opening	$ 250			$ 250
Morning	$ 180			$ 180
Breakout Sessions (sum of Session 1, Session 2, and Session 3)	$ 300			$ 300
Session 1	$ 100			$ 100
Session 2	$ 100			$ 100
Session 3	$ 100			$ 100
Closing	$ 150			$ 150

Each work package has an appropriate dollar amount associated with it. You will also want to keep track of how the estimates were derived and how robust the numbers are. For example, if you asked for three quotes on how much the location would cost and you took the high quote, be sure to maintain the supporting documentation. Your sponsor or your organization's accounting and finance team may request documentation as to how cost estimates were derived.

Please note that you may discover that your project exceeds the upper limit as to what your sponsor was willing to spend on the project. If this occurs, review your data to make sure that it is accurate and that you are spending only what is required to deliver the project. After you have double-checked yourself, you should then ask your sponsor for further guidance. After reviewing your work, your sponsor may be fine with the additional spending or may have some thoughts as to how to reduce the cost. In either case, you never want to surprise your sponsor by going over the budget.

Work Package	Cost	Source of the Estimate
Conference	**$ 3,530**	
Location	$ 1,600	
Building	*$ 1,000*	*Obtained quotes from 3 vendors*
Parking	*$ 250*	*Obtained from city*
Security	*$ 350*	*Used published industry rates*
Meals	**$ 1,050**	
Breakfast	*$ 350*	*Obtained quotes from 3 caterers*
Lunch	*$ 550*	*Obtained quotes from 3 caterers*
Snacks	*$ 150*	*Created a grocery list to buy from local store*
Program	**$ 880**	
Opening	*$ 250*	*Market value of Speaker Honoria*
Morning	*$ 180*	*Market value of Speaker Honoria*
Breakout Sessions	*$ 300*	

Work Package	Cost	Source of the Estimate
Session 1	$ 100	Organizational Policy
Session 2	$ 100	Organizational Policy
Session 3	$ 100	Organizational Policy
Closing	*$ 150*	*Speaker's Market Value*

RISK PLANNING

As you work on completing your project plan, you need to plan for all of the things that can go wrong as well as right on your project. This is called *risk planning*. Risk planning can compensate for a poor project plan, as you will address issues that can possibly interfere with delivering the project.

Risk is an unplanned event that may or may not occur and will have either a positive or negative impact on the project. Basically, you will list all of the risks that have the potential to harm (or help) the project. Then you'll develop a plan to reduce the impact upon your project.

Your project team should help you develop the risk plan. Ask them to list all of the problems that may occur. While you can clarify the risks, do not spend too much time on discussing strategies at this time or even the merits of the identified risk. Simply note the risk; you will discuss them later in the process. After you have listed multiple risks, note the likelihood (probability) of the occurrence and the consequence (impact) if it were to occur. Use a 1 to 5 ranking, with 1 being the least likely to occur and having the least impact. A 5 will denote that it is very likely that the risk will occur and that the impact to the project will be severe. After you have analyzed all of the risks, multiply your scores for probability and impact and then rank order them with the highest score at the top of your list. You will then spend the greater amount of time discussing mitigating strategies for the higher ones and less time on the lower-ranking risks.

Some of the mitigating strategies will not have a cost associated with them. For example, the alternative speaker may be someone from within the company that is put on standby in case a speaker does not show up. Likewise, there may not be an additional cost in doing the food tasting with the vendor as part of the preparations. On the other hand, the additional projector and buses to transport individuals in the event that an overflow parking lot is used may mean that additional costs will have to be factored into the budget. Just make sure that the amount to compensate for the risks is commensurate with the risks. Working with your sponsor, you may want to include these potential additional costs in your budget. This way if the risk were to occur, you will have the funds on hand to deal with the issue.

While we tend to focus on the things that can go wrong (negative risks), it is possible for things to go better than expected (positive risks).

Negative Risks	Probability (1-5)	Impact (1-5)	P*I	Ranking	Mitigating Strategy
The projector does not work	3	5	15	1	Have a second projector and backup laptop ready with the speaker notes backed up on a CD
Speaker does not show up	2	5	10	2	Have an alternative speaker ready
The meals are not very good	3	3	9	3	Have a food tasting as part of the vendor analysis
There is not enough parking	1	2	2	4	Have overflow parking spaces with buses to transport attendees to the event site

Positive Risks	Probability (1-5)	Impact (1-5)	P*I	Ranking	Mitigating Strategy
More attendees come than expected (They heard what a great conference this will be.)	4	5	20	1	Have a set of overflow rooms at another hotel to accommodate the additional attendees. Have a plan to add more chairs to the breakout session rooms if necessary.
Attendees really want more information from a particular speaker	4	3	12	2	Work with your IT department to put up an internal blog site on the company intranet so that speakers can engage their audience after the conference.
The meals are outstanding	3	3	9	3	Be sure to thank the hotel staff for outstanding service.

CONNECTING THE DOTS

At this stage you have defined the scope, created the schedule, incorporated the budget, and thought about some of the risks that can positively or negatively impact your project. Now you need to integrate all of the pieces together into a cohesive project plan. The integrated plan may be a Word document that looks like the Scope-Time-Responsibility-Cost (STRaC) Matrix below.

Once this is established and published, if one of the constraints (scope schedule, cost) changes, then one or both of the other constraints must also change. For example, if another activity is added and it has been approved by the change control board, then the cost and perhaps the schedule will change.

Work Package (Scope)	Due Date (Time)	Team Member (Responsibility)	Cost Estimate (Cost)
Conference	*March 1*	*Jack*	*$ 3,530*
Location	January 25	Jerry	$ 1,600
Building	January 15	*Mike*	*$ 1,000*
Parking	January 20	*Mary*	*$ 250*
Security	January 25	*Lou*	*$ 350*
Meals	February 1	Julie	$ 1,050
Breakfast	February 1	*Ann*	*$ 350*
Lunch	February 1	*John*	*$ 550*
Snacks	February 1	*Joe*	*$ 150*
Program	March 1	Mary	$ 880
Opening	March 1	*Al*	*$ 250*
Morning	March 1	*Charles*	*$ 180*
Breakout Sessions	March 1	*Frank*	*$ 300*
Session 1	March 1	Andre	$ 100
Session 2	March 1	Teresa	$ 100
Session 3	March 1	Tammy	$ 100
Closing	March 1	*Alex*	*$ 150*

REVIEW THE PLAN AND WORK THE PLAN

Congratulations, you are ready to have a kick-off meeting with your team to review the project plan and begin executing. At this point it becomes a leadership challenge. Success and failure on a project is oftentimes determined by how well you lead the project—after all, the project will not get done unless you proactively follow through on the plan. Go to **www.tmogllc. com/PMQuickStart** for a brief paper on the "Leadership Expectations of a Project Manager." Execute the plan by continuously monitoring and updating your work schedule as you progress. Keep track of your costs, as you will at some point have to account for all of the monies that have been spent. Do not forget that with each work package there is some set of quality expectations that has to be met before the work package can be considered complete.

Each day, review the following:

- Any new stakeholders? If there are new stakeholders, ask yourself, what are their requirements, and do I need to increase or decrease the scope? If the scope changes, what are the impacts to the schedule and cost?

- Any new risks? If new risks appear, ask yourself the same questions.

- At key points, obtain appropriate updates and publish the updates.

- Keep up with the "good" things that folks do by creating a drop file.

- As each work package is completed, do a mini–lessons learned.

Closing out a project can be a project in itself. In the case of our conference project, the project is not over when the last guest goes home—the project is complete when the *lessons learned* has been completed and all of the obligations have been settled.

- Make sure that each work package is completed to standard and that the customer is satisfied with the results.

- Complete your financial obligations. Make sure that the subcontractors have been paid. If you have internal employees that were a part of the project, you may also want to provide performance feedback to their functional managers.

- Do a lessons learned for the entire project and publish it. You should do this even if the project was a resounding success. It is important to capture best practices that can be implemented on future projects. Likewise, if the project was a troubled one (i.e., over budget, behind schedule), you still need to do a lessons learned.

- CELEBRATE! It does not have to be much, but it should be something. Too often, we just go from project to project, but take a few minutes to celebrate the closure of a project with your key project team members.

OTHER THOUGHTS

Running a project is hard work. Rarely will you have enough money and time to do everything that everyone wants done on the project. Leading and managing projects is not for everyone. But it is rewarding and a much-sought-after skill in today's world. Just know that it is only by taking on the tough assignments and working on your skill sets that you will become proficient in delivering successful projects.

For more information regarding some of the key words used throughout the writing, you can reference the Project Management Institute A guide to the Project Management Body of Knowledge (PMBOK® Guide) - Fifth Edition, Project Management Institute, Inc., 2013. Copyright and all rights reserved. Materials used from this publication have been reproduced with the permission of PMI.

You will find some additional templates at **www.tmogllc.com/PMQuickStart**. These templates will help you to organize your project.

Best of luck in all of your endeavors, and do stay in touch!

PMBOK is a registered mark of the Project Management Institute, Inc.

ABOUT THE AUTHOR

Jon McGlothian, MBA, CMA, PMP | Principal | TMOG, LLC

Jon McGlothian is the cofounder and president of TMOG, LLC. As a graduate of West Point, he completed his service with Third Ranger Battalion. He earned the Bronze Star for meritorious actions while serving his country. After earning his MBA from the University of Memphis, he was awarded the Kurt Christoff Award for being the outstanding MBA student of the year. In 2005, The University of Memphis honored Jon as the Young Alumni of the Year for outstanding contributions to the university and community. He is also a Project Management Professional (PMP)® as well as a Certified Management Accountant (CMA) and is a certified Six Sigma

---

PMP is a registered mark of the Project Management Institute, Inc.

Green Belt. He has also held several executive positions at Fortune 500 companies. He has taught a variety of business and leadership courses at a local university and is a contributor for the *Project Management Body of Knowledge* (PMBOK® Guide) – Fifth Edition, Project Management Institute, Inc., 2013.

He and his family currently reside in Virginia Beach, Virginia, where he actively serves on several nonprofit boards.

Jon brings to bear his experience as an officer in the US Army Ranger Regiment, a Fortune 500 company executive, an entrepreneur, and a community leader to this effort. He is highly dedicated to developing leaders who can manage, deliver the job, and be an inspiration to others.

Physical Address:
4968 Euclid Road | Suite D | Virginia Beach, VA 23462

Mailing Address:
PO Box 56415 | Virginia Beach, VA 23456
Direct: 757-559-1566 | Fax: 757-271-1598
jon@tmogllc.com | www.tmogllc.com

About TMOG, LLC

TMOG, LLC specializes in providing project management training and consulting for the Department of Defense as well as government agencies and corporate entities.

Project Management Institute (PMI), the world's largest project management member association, has named TMOG, LLC as a Registered Education Provider (R.E.P.). R.E.P.s are organizations that have been approved by PMI to help project managers achieve and maintain their PMI professional credentials. These organizations have met PMI's rigorous quality criteria for course content, instructor qualification, and instructional design.

Project managers are increasingly turning to R.E.P.s for certification training and maintenance, especially since median salaries for the profession now exceed $100,000 (USD).